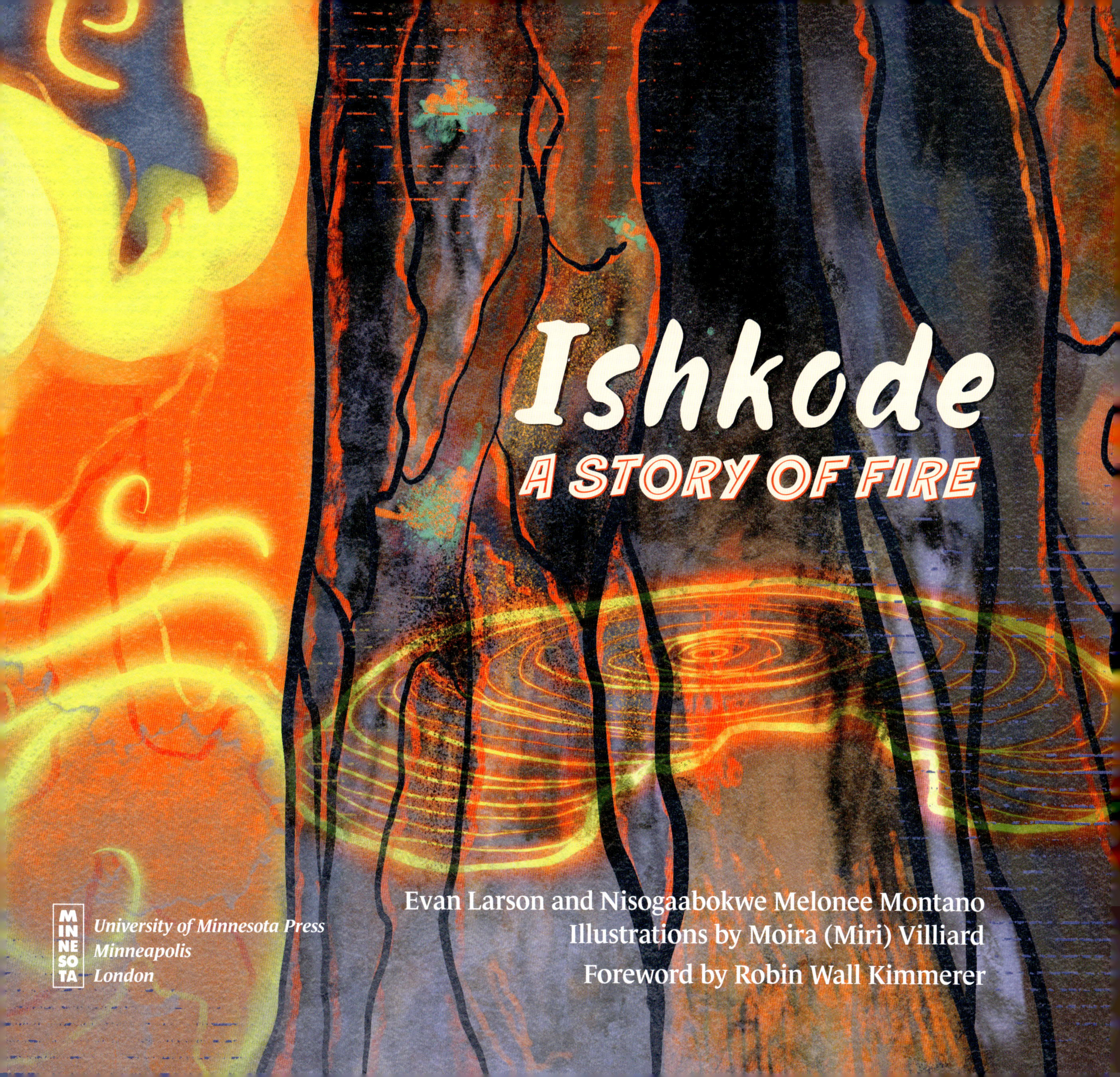

Ishkode

A Story of Fire

Evan Larson and Nisogaabokwe Melonee Montano
Illustrations by Moira (Miri) Villiard
Foreword by Robin Wall Kimmerer

MINNESOTA
University of Minnesota Press
Minneapolis
London

Foreword

Yatsokejek gechwa mnedowiwat—
Storytellers are sacred. They connect us to the lives of the past, helping us remember to remember. We owe a debt of gratitude to the ones who keep our stories alive. Words hold stories too, in the deep meaning of our languages and the lessons they hold for us.

The land is full of stories, illustrated in rock and soil, sung by birds, and written in the rings of trees. They are the scribes of the forest. Tree ring stories share history as well as guidance. Stories stretch our imagination of what the future can be, for we are also storymakers.

In Anishinaabe thought, stories are understood as living entities. They grow and change and emerge when we need them. We need the stories told by the pines, by the blueberries, by the scientists and the elders. I am grateful for the gift of this lovely book, which brings their stories to light. May we listen to them closely.

—Robin Wall Kimmerer

Mewinzha, long ago . . .

a family of *bapakwanagemagoog*, red pine trees, lived on a point of *aki*, land, reaching out into a *zaaga'igan*, lake. Some of the *bapakwanagemagoog* were younger than twenty years, while others were hundreds of years old. Their trunks reached for *giizhig*, the sky, to bring branches and needles into the wind and light where they feasted on sunshine.

Each year the *mitigoog*, trees, used energy from *giizis*, sun, and *nibi*, water, and nutrients from *aki* to write *dibaajimowinan*, stories, of the forest as annual growth rings. Years when *giizis* was bright and rains abundant were recorded as wide rings, while droughts or long winters and short summers were etched as narrow rings.

Set within this *dibaajimowin*, story, of rains and drought were curving lines of dark resin—scars that marked years when *ishkode*, fire, passed by the *mitigoog* and heated their bodies in a process of reciprocal renewal. The *mitigoog* offered their needles to *ishkode*, who in return cleared *aki* and created places for *abinoojiinyensag*, babies, the next generation of *bapakwanagemag* to take root and grow.

"Oh! *Noozhishenh!* This is a good place to pick *miinan.*"

The *mitigoog* were not alone on the point. Beneath their open arms and canopies, nestled among baby *bapakwanagemagoog,* were widely spread *miinagaawanzhiig*, blueberry bushes, with branches full of *miinan,* blueberries!

At the very tip of the point, where *nibi* meets *aki*, stood *Aanikoobijigan*, an ancient Grandmother *bapakwanagemag*. Her body was twisted and bent from a life that spanned centuries of wind, *ishkode*, droughts, and rains; years of hardship, loss, renewal, and growth among her family. She remembered the *dibaajimowinan* of others, too, including the *Anishinaabeg* who came to harvest *miinan* when the *Miini-giizis*, Blueberry Moon, shined brightly in the sky.

This year, like so many before, she heard the forest sharing news of a *Nookomis*, grandmother, accompanied by her *Noozhishenh,* granddaughter, who were approaching the point.

Aanikoobijigan stood still and waited as the *Anishinaabeg* offered *asemaa*, their sacred tobacco, and a spirit dish to the *manidoog*, spirits, and then began to harvest. As the people moved from bush to bush, picking *miinan* just like *makwa*, bear, *Aanikoobijigan* listened for a *dibaajimowin* that she had heard the *Anishinaabeg* tell many times before, *dibaajimowin* that she remembered within her body, among her rings laid down year after year.

As they moved across the point, *Nookomis* noticed the attention of *Noozhishenh* was wandering from the task of picking *miinan*. Looking on with a smile, she spoke.

"Come *Noozhishenh*, I will tell you a *dibaajimowin* as we pick."

Mewinzha, the people were cold and hungry, for they had no *ishkode* to keep them warm.

Nearby, *Aandeg*, crow, splendid in *miigwanag*, feathers, that carried all the colors of *nagweyaab*, the rainbow, and with a voice as beautiful in *nagamon*, song, as any other, saw this and decided to let the Creator know about the suffering of the people.

Once he shared this news with the Creator, the Creator offered up some *ishkode* from his *wiigiwaam*, lodge.

Aandeg agreed to take *ishkode* and give it as a gift to the people.

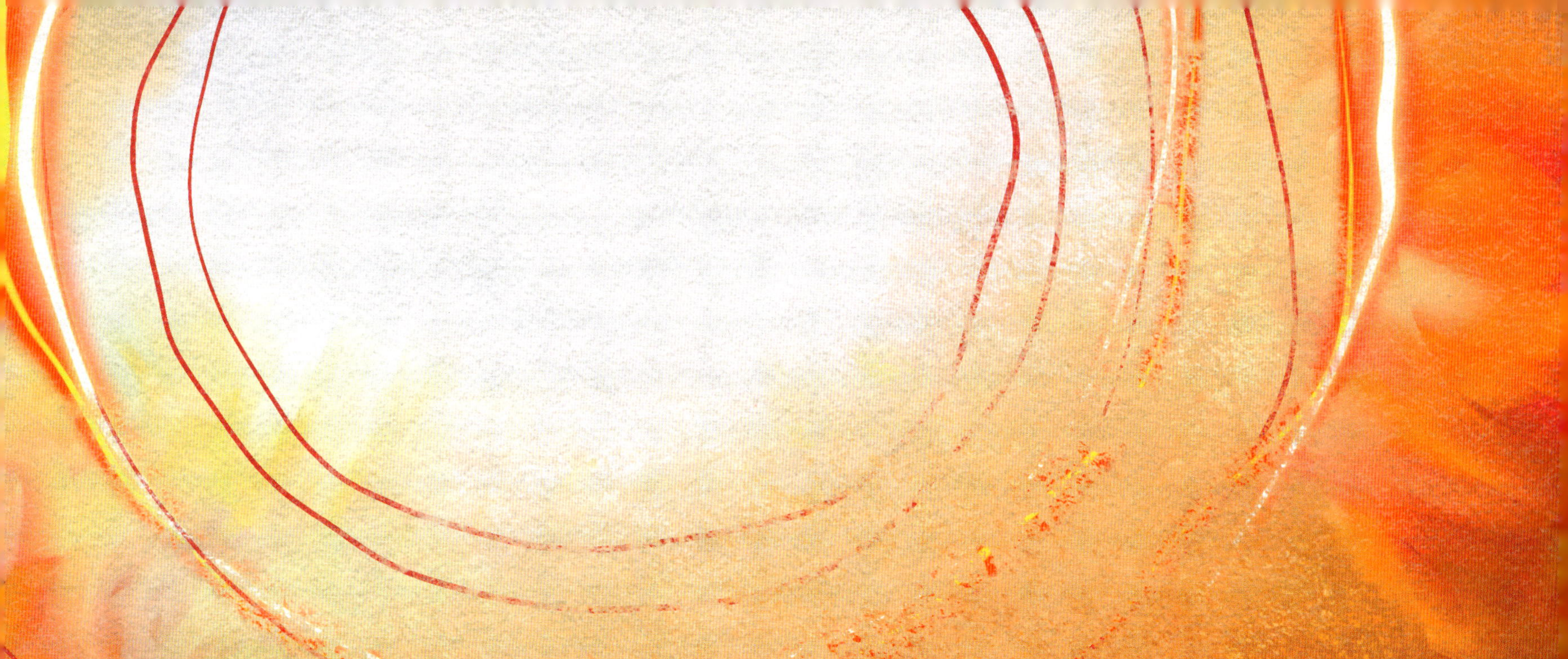

Aandeg carried *ishkode* as a burning branch down to *aki*, and as he flew the heat from *ishkode* burned hotter and began to scorch *Aandeg's* beautiful *miigwanag*. He called to the *Anishinaabeg*, to let them know he was coming and flew faster.

By the time he arrived in the village, the flames of *ishkode* had blackened his *miigwanag*, and when he shared the news of *ishkode* with the *Anishinaabeg*, his voice came out harsh and croaking, for the flames had burned his throat.

Still, he shared how *ishkode* could help the people, keep them warm, cook *miijim*, their food, and help them care for *aki* so that *aki*, in return, would care for the people. He also warned that if the people ignored or disrespected this *miigiwewin*, gift, it would leave, or worse, become harmful.

Aandeg did all of this for the *Anishinaabeg*—he sacrificed his beauty and his *nagamon* for the good of the people. To know this is true, all you need to do is look at the *miigwanag* of *Aandeg* in the light of *giizis* and see that beneath the black they still shimmer with all the colors of the *nagweyaab*.

And so it is our responsibility to continue following these instructions and to care for our relatives in the future.

The *dibaajimowin* ended, and as *Nookomis* looked first at the *makak*, basket, now full to the brim with *miinan*, and then at *Noozhishenh*, she nodded.

"There are *miinan* left, but those are for others. This is enough. *Miigwech.*"

As the people prepared to leave the point, a light breeze blew from the east. The breeze drifted through the branches of the *bapakwanagemagoog* and shook free dry needles, which fell and caught among the branches of the *miinagaawanzhiig*. Seeing this and recognizing it was the right time, *Nookomis* turned, kneeled, and with thanks in her heart, she set alight *ishkode* on the point.

Ishkode slowly spread across the point, murmuring thanks while consuming the needles of the *bapakwanagemagoog* and old branches of the *miinagaawanzhiig*. The *miinagaawanzhiig* celebrated, knowing the flames would lead to new sprouts and rejuvenation. *Bapakwanagemagoog* welcomed the flames, too, for *aki* was now open and receptive to *miinikaanan*, their seeds, and *aanikoobijiganag*, their ancestors. As *ishkode* gently passed her trunk in this process of renewal and reciprocity, *Aanikoobijigan* wrote the *dibaajimowin* in her rings.

The next year, as *Miini-giizis* brightened the night *giizhig* and *miinan* ripened in the long hours of late summer sunlight filtering down through the open branches of the *bapakwanagemagoog*, *Aanikoobijigan* looked for the people and listened for their *dibaajimowinan*.

But no *Anishinaabe* came, and no *dibaajimowinan* were told. Nor did they come the next year . . . Nor the next.

In the absence of *ishkode*, the forest grew denser and denser. The *miinagaawanzhiig* diminished in the deepening shade and the *bapakwanagemagoog* found no place for their *miinikaanan*, *abinoojiinyag*, their children.

Then a rumor came through the woods. People were back, but they spoke with different voices and sang different *nagamonan*, songs . . .

. . . and they took everything.

Except *Aanikoobijigan*, whose body was too bent and twisted to be worth cutting.

Done with the point, the new people did not return.

A drought arrived, though, and hot *ishkode* raged through the branches and bodies of the *bapakwanagemagoog* left behind, consuming the soil and the *miinikaanan* of their next generation . . .

. . . and *Aanikoobijigan* recorded the *dibaajimowin* in her rings.

Many years later and not long ago, an *oshkiniigikwe*, a young woman, named *Animikiimiikanikwe* arrived at the point. The forest had changed, and *Aanikoobijigan* now lingered alone among her new neighbors, her *miinikaanan* falling only to wither in shade.

Animikiimiikanikwe had read about her *aanikoobijiganag*, and how they had lived on and with *aki*.

Determined to know the places where her people had walked and lived, she began searching for connections with the past. A *dibaajimowin* from her *aanikoobijigan* had described a point of land with *bapakwanagemagoog* and *miinan*, leading her here.

As *Animikiimiikanikwe* approached the tip of the point where *nibi* meets *aki*, she could feel the history of the place. Just then, a breeze blew from the east, drifting through the branches of *Aanikoobijigan*, and across the cheek of the *oshkiniigikwe*. Within that breath, a single cluster of needles fell to rest among the twigs of an old *miinagaawanzh*.

The movement of the falling needles caught *Animikiimiikanikwe*'s eye and drew her attention to a tiny, dry *miin*, blueberry, clinging to a branch of the bush. At the sight of the berry, memories flooded back to *Animikiimiikanikwe*. She remembered her *Nookomis*, and the *dibaajimowin* she told about picking *miinan* with her own *Nookomis* on a point of land just like this. She remembered the delicious *miini-baashkiminasigani-biitoosijigani-bakwezhiganag*, blueberry pies, that her *Nookomis* baked and the careful gratitude of her hands as she served each piece.

An overwhelming sadness filled *Animikiimiikanikwe*. She missed her *Nookomis*, yet felt a more profound hurt of broken relationships and lost connection. Tears welling in her eyes, the *oshkiniigikwe* reeled under the weight of these feelings, only to find the support of rough *wanagek*, bark, on her back. In the embrace of *Aanikoobijigan*'s curving trunk, *Animikiimiikanikwe* lowered herself to *aki*, where, cradled by roots of the ancient *mitig*, tree, she cried herself to sleep and into *bawaajigan*, a dream.

In her *bawaajigan*, *Animikiimiikanikwe* stood on the point next to *Aanikoobijigan* and reached her arms to *giizhig*.

A wind rose from the east, and on it roiled *anakwadoon*, clouds, with *Animikii*, Thunderbird, in their midst. The storm swept over the point, raging against all the loss across generations, the pain, and the hurt, with lightning flashing and *animikiikaa*, thunder, rolling. With a tremendous crash, a brilliant bolt of lightning struck *Aanikoobijigan*. Her body split as she fell to *aki*.

In her *bawaajigan*, *Animikiimiikanikwe* turned to mourn the passing of the ancient *mitig*. In doing so she noticed distinct marks etched within the body of *Aanikoobijigan*. Tucked within the growth rings of her long life were dark lines of boiled resin that recorded each passing of *ishkode* that she had witnessed. In that moment, *Animikiimiikanikwe* understood that these marks, these scars from *ishkode*, were the *dibaajimowinan* of her *aanikoobijiganag*, carried over centuries and across generations by *Aanikoobijigan*, to help the people remember.

When *Animikiimiikanikwe* woke from her *bawaajigan*, the *dibaajimowin* from *Aanikoobijigan* was clear in her memory. She offered *asemaa* for the *bawaajigan* and walked away from the point, knowing her purpose and that she would one day return.

Shortly after, as *Miini-Giizis* again brightened the sky, *Animikiimiikanikwe* returned with family, community, and *aanikoobijiganag*. Together, they began the work of rebuilding their relationships with *aki* and the *bapakwanagemagoog*.

After days of effort, all was ready, and the time was right. *Animikiimiikanikwe* knelt, offered *asemaa*, and with thanks in her heart, she set alight *ishkode* on the point. The flames moved gently over the land, leaving a wake of renewal in their path. The stunted *miinagaawanzh*, with sweetened soil and space to grow, looked ahead to days of *giizis* and *miinan*, and as *ishkode* wove around her trunk, *Aanikoobijigan* smiled, and wrote the *dibaajimowin* in her rings.

Ojibwe Pronunciation Guide

For this book, we have chosen to use the double vowel system commonly used today when writing in the *Ojibwe* language. Below is information intended to be used as a guide to pronouncing the *Ojibwe* words.

Note that the only **nasal vowel** used in this book is "enh." Vowels in a word are nasalized before the letters ns, nz, and nzh. Also, long vowels (aa, e, ii, oo) after a nasal consonant (n or m) are often nasalized, especially when they come before s, sh, z, or zh. In addition, between the letters h and i in the Ojibwe alphabet is an apostrophe ('), which is a symbol used for a glottal stop.

Ojibwe Alphabet

a, aa, b, c, d, e, g, h, ', i, ii, j, k, m, n, o, oo, p, s, t, w, y, z

Vowel Type	Vowel	Ojibwe Example	English Example
Short	a	m**a**kw**a**	s**u**n
Long	aa	**aa**ndeg	s**o**ng
Long	e	as**e**maa	s**a**cred
Short	i	**i**shkode	spir**i**ts
Long	ii	animik**ii**kaa	s**ee**ds
Short	o	**o**shkiniigikwe	tobacc**o**
Long	oo	n**oo**komis	bl**ue**berry
Nasal	aanh	banaj**aanh**	
Nasal	enh	noozhish**enh**	
Nasal	iinh	awes**iinh**	
Nasal	oonh	giig**oonh**	

Ojibwe words used in this book

Aandeg – *Crow*

Aanikoobijigan / Aanikoobijiganag – *Great Grandchild, Great Grandparent, Ancestor / Great Grandchildren, Great Grandparents, Ancestors*

Abinoojiinyensag – *Babies*

Aki – *Earth, Ground, Land*

Anakwadoon – *Clouds*

Animikii – *Thunderbird*

Animikiikaa – *Thunder*

Asemaa – *Sacred Tobacco*

Bapakwanagemag / Bapakwanagemagoog – *Red Pine Tree / Red Pine Trees*

Bawaajigan – *Dream*

Dibaajimowin / Dibaajimowinan – *Story / Stories*

Gichi-aya'aag – *Elders*

Giizhig – *Sky*

Giizis – *Sun*

Gikendaasowin – *Knowledge*

Inwewin – *Language*

Ishkode – *Fire*

Makwa – *Bear*

Manidoog – *Spirits*

Mewinzha – *Long ago*

Miigiwewin – *Gift*

Miigwanag – *Feathers*

Miigwech – *Thank you*

Miijim – *Food*

Makak – *Basket*

Miin / Miinan – *Blueberry / Blueberries*

Miinagaawanzh / Miinagaawanzhiig – *Blueberry plant / Blueberry plants*

Miini-baashkiminasigani-biitoosijigani-bakwezhiganag – *Blueberry Pie*

Miini-giizis – *Blueberry Moon*

Miinikaanan – *Seeds*

Mitig / Mitigoog – *Tree / Trees*

Nagamon / Nagamonan – *Song / Songs*

Nagweyaab – *Rainbow*

Nibi – *Water*

Nookomis – *Grandmother*

Noozhishenh – *Grandchild*

Oshkiniigikwe – *Young Woman / Adolescent Girl*

Wanagek – *Bark*

Wiigiwaam – *Lodge*

Zaaga'igan – *Lake*

About the Creators

EVAN LARSON is a father, husband, professor, and enthusiast of trees, fires, and wild places. Growing up in central Minnesota with sawdust and twigs in his hair set the stage, and since first looking through a microscope at tree rings and fire scars in the summer of 2001, the science of dendrochronology and the wisdom of trees have profoundly shaped Evan's life in ways that he is still coming to understand. Evan lives in Platteville, Wisconsin, with his wife Danica, their two daughters, an assortment of furry creatures, and a wild lawn that on occasion burns, much to the celebration of the plants who live there.

NISOGAABOKWE MELONEE MONTANO is a mother, grandmother, and enrolled member of the Red Cliff Band of Lake Superior Chippewa. She is owner of Ethical Embers LLC, a company that guides individuals, communities, and organizations in incorporating Indigenous knowledges and practices into land management efforts. Throughout her life, her employment and education have focused on learning about and caring for the environment through Indigenous and Western scientific lenses. Most recently, she turned to fire as one of her teachers and, therefore, is committed to learning all she can to help return fire to landscapes. Lastly and most importantly, she is a lifelong student of her cultural ways.

Through public art collaborations across Minnesota, **MOIRA (MIRI) VILLIARD** is a multidisciplinary artist who uses art to uplift underrepresented narratives, explore the nuance of society's historical community intersections, and promote community healing spaces. Her areas of focus include responsive/protest art, community space curation, illustration, activism-rooted exhibitions, animated projection art, and participatory murals. Moira descends from a long family history rooted deeply in the Great Lakes region; she grew up on the Fond du Lac Reservation in Cloquet, Minnesota, and is a Fond du Lac Ojibwe direct descendant. Her overall work seeks to bridge gaps in community memory and recognition.

ROBIN WALL KIMMERER is author of several books, including *Braiding Sweetgrass: Indigenous Wisdom, Scientific Knowledge, and the Teachings of Plants* and *The Serviceberry: Abundance and Reciprocity in the Natural World.*

Acknowledgments

The writing of this book was made possible by the generous wisdom of *mitigoog*, trees, and the *dibaajimowinan*, stories, they write in annual growth rings every year of their lives. We acknowledge the *bapakwanagemagoog*, red pine trees, as our *gichi-aya'aag*, elders, and teachers, and thank them for carrying the *dibaajimowin*, story, of *ishkode*, fire, across generations. Translating this *gikendaasowin*, knowledge, from the *inwewin*, language, of *mitigoog* to the *inwewin* of people was guided by the science of dendrochronology.

For more information about the science and stories behind this book, please visit www.ishkode.org.